Book of Devotions

Pocket Size Edition

*Compiled
by
Joseph Coppolino*

ST PAULS

Nihil Obstat:
    James T. O'Connor, S.T.D.
    Censor Librorum

Imprimatur:
    Joseph T. O'Keefe, D.D.
    Vicar General
    Archdiocese of New York
    December 20, 1985

The Nihil Obstat and Imprimatur are a declaration that a book or pamphlet is considered to be free from doctrinal or moral error. It is not implied that those who have granted the Nihil Obstat and Imprimatur agree with the contents, opinions or statements expressed.

ISBN:0-8189-0503-4

Designed, printed and bound
in the United States of America
by the Fathers and Brothers of the
Society of St. Paul,
2187 Victory Boulevard,
Staten Island, New York 10314,
as part of their communications apostolate.

© Copyright 2001 by the Society of St. Paul

Current printing — first digit   1   2   3   4   5   6   7   8   9

Year of current printing — first year shown
2001   2002   2003   2004   2005   2006   2007   2008

Contents

Sign of the Cross 7
The Our Father 7
The Hail Mary 7
The Glory Be 7
The Apostles' Creed 8
The Angelus 8
Act of Adoration 9
Act of Faith 9
Act of Hope 10
Act of Love 10
Act of Contrition 10
Prayer of Thanksgiving 11
For the Souls in Purgatory 11
For the Dying 11
For Vocations 11
Prayer Before Meals 12
Prayer After Meals 12
To the Guardian Angel 12
Act of Consecration to the
    Immaculate Heart of Mary 12
Morning Offering 13
Blue Army Pledge 13
Formula of The Heroic Act of Love 14
Prayer for Poor Sinners 15

Eucharistic Prayer 15
Rosary Decade Prayer 15
Prayer for Pardon 16
Sacrifice Prayer 16
Prayer for Mercy 16
Prayer to our Blessed Mother 17
The Fifteen Prayers as revealed by
    Our Lord to Saint Bridget 18
Salutation of the Wound
    in the Shoulder of Jesus 27
Invocation in honor of the Holy
    Wounds of Our Lord Jesus Christ 28
Prayer to Jesus Crucified 28
Anima Christi 29
To Our Lord on the Cross 29
Act of Consecration to the Sacred Heart of Jesus 30
Veni, Creator 31
Magnificat 32
Ave, Maris Stella 33
Litany of the Holy Spirit 34
Litany of the Blessed Virgin 37
Litany of the Holy Name of Jesus 40
Litany of the Sacred Heart of Jesus 43
Litany of Saint Joseph 46
Prayer to Saint Joseph 48
Saint Joseph, Patron of Workers 49
Saint Joseph, Chaste Spouse of Mary 50

An Illustrated Book of Devotions 5

Prayer for Virginity 51
Prayer for Purity 51
For A Happy Death 52
O Jesus, Living in Mary 52
Prayers from The Little Office of the Immaculate
  Conception of the Blessed Virgin Mary 53
The New Secret of Salvation 64
The Rosary 71
The Way of the Cross 103
The Perpetual Novena in honor of Our Lady of the
  Miraculous Medal 135
The Chaplet of the Divine Mercy 142

The Holy Family

Most Popular Common Prayers

Sign of the Cross

In the name of the Father, and of the Son, and of the Holy Spirit. Amen.

The Our Father

Our Father, Who art in Heaven, hallowed be Thy name. Thy kingdom come; Thy will be done, on earth as it is in Heaven. Give us this day our daily bread and forgive us our trespasses as we forgive those who trespass against us. And lead us not into temptation but deliver us from evil. Amen.

The Hail Mary

Hail Mary, full of grace, the Lord is with you. Blessed are you among women and blessed is the fruit of your womb, Jesus. Holy Mary, Mother of God, pray for us sinners, now and at the hour of our death. Amen.

The Glory Be

Glory be to the Father, and to the Son, and to the Holy Spirit, as it was in the beginning, is now and ever shall be, world without end. Amen.

The Apostles' Creed

I believe in God, the Father almighty, Creator of heaven and earth; and in Jesus Christ, His only Son, our Lord: who was conceived by the Holy Spirit, born of the Virgin Mary, suffered under Pontius Pilate, was crucified, died and was buried. He descended into hell; the third day He rose again from the dead. He ascended into heaven and sits at the right hand of God, the Father almighty; from thence He shall come to judge the living and the dead. I believe in the Holy Spirit, the holy Catholic Church, the communion of saints, the forgiveness of sins, the resurrection of the body, and life everlasting. Amen.

The Angelus

V. The angel of God spoke God's message to Mary.
R. And she conceived of the Holy Spirit.
    Hail Mary....
V. Behold the handmaid of the Lord.
R. Be it done unto me according to your word.
    Hail Mary....
V. And the Word was made flesh.
R. And dwelt among us.
    Hail Mary....

V. Pray for us, O holy Mother of God.
R. That we may be made worthy of the promises of Christ.

Let us pray.

Pour forth, we beseech You, O Lord, Your grace into our hearts that we, to whom the Incarnation of Christ, Your Son, was made known by the message of an angel may, by His passion and death, be brought to the glory of His resurrection, through the same Christ our Lord. Amen.

Act of Adoration

I adore You, my God, and I love You with all my heart. I thank You for having created me, made me a Christian, and kept me safe this night (day). I offer You all that I think, or say or do and ask that they may be according to Your most holy will and for Your greater glory. Keep me from all sin and evil. May Your grace be always with me and with all my loved ones. Amen.

Act of Faith

O my God, I firmly believe that You are one God in three Divine Persons: Father, Son and Holy Spirit. I believe that your Divine Son became man and died for our sins, and that He will come again to judge the living and the dead. I believe these and all the truths which the holy Catholic Church teaches, because You have revealed them, Who can neither deceive nor be deceived. Amen.

Act of Hope

O my God, relying on Your infinite goodness and promises, I hope to obtain pardon for my sins, the help of Your grace, and life everlasting, through the merits of Jesus Christ, my Lord and Redeemer. Amen.

Act of Love

O my God, I love You above all things, with my whole heart and soul, because You are all good and worthy of all my love. I love my neighbor as myself for love of You. I forgive all who have injured me and ask pardon of all whom I have injured. Amen.

Act of Contrition

O my God, I am heartily sorry for having offended You. I detest all my sins because of Your just punishments, but most of all because they have offended

You, my God, Who are all good and deserving of all my love. I firmly resolve, with the help of Your grace, to confess my sins, to do penance and to avoid the near occasions of sin in the future. Lord, have mercy on me a sinner. Amen.

Prayer of Thanksgiving

We give You thanks, almighty God, for all Your gifts, Who lives and reigns forever and ever. Amen.

For the Souls in Purgatory

Eternal rest grant unto them, O Lord, and let perpetual light shine upon them. May they rest in peace. Amen.

For the Dying

St. Joseph, foster father of Jesus Christ and true spouse of the Virgin Mary, pray for us and for the dying of this day. Amen.

For Vocations

Jesus, eternal Shepherd of our souls, send good laborers into Your harvest. Amen.

Prayer Before Meals

Bless us, O Lord, and these Your gifts which we are about to receive from Your bounty through Christ our Lord. Amen.

Prayer After Meals

We give You thanks, O Lord, for the food we have just received. Grant that it may sustain us in Your holy service. Amen.

To the Guardian Angel

Angel of God, my guardian dear, to whom God's love entrusts me here, ever this day be at my side, to light and guard, to rule and guide. Amen.

Act of Consecration to the Immaculate Heart of Mary

(St. Louis de Montfort's Consecration)

I, N., a faithless sinner, renew and ratify today in your hands, O Immaculate Mother, the vows of my Baptism; I renounce forever Satan, his pomps and works; and I give myself entirely to Jesus Christ, the Incarnate Wisdom, to carry my cross after Him all the days of my life, and to be more faithful to Him than I have ever been before.

In the presence of all the heavenly court I choose you this day for my Mother and Mistress. I deliver and consecrate to you, as your slave, my body and soul, my goods, both interior and exterior, and even the value of all my good actions, past, present and future; leaving to you the entire and full right of disposing of me, and all that belongs to me, without exception, according to your good pleasure, for the greater glory of God, in time and in eternity. Amen.

Morning Offering

O my Jesus, through the Immaculate Heart of Mary I offer You all my prayers, works, joys, and sufferings of this day, in union with the Holy Sacrifice of the Mass throughout the world, in reparation for all my sins, for the intention of our Holy Father the Pope, the poor souls in Purgatory, the conversion of sinners, and the reign of Your Sacred Heart and the Immaculate Heart of Mary throughout the world. Amen.

Blue Army Pledge

O my God, in union with the Immaculate Heart of Mary (here kiss your Brown Scapular as a sign of your consecration), I offer You the Precious Blood of Jesus united with His most Sacred Wounds from all the altars throughout the world, joining with It the offering of my every thought, word and action of this day. Amen.

O my Jesus, I desire today to gain every indulgence and merit I can, united with Your most Sacred Wounds and I offer them, together with myself, to Mary Immaculate, that she may best apply them to the interests of Your most Sacred Heart. Precious Blood of Jesus, save us! Immaculate Heart of Mary, pray for us! Sacred Heart of Jesus, have mercy on us! Amen.

Formula of The Heroic Act of Love

O Holy and Adorable Trinity, desiring to cooperate in the deliverance of the souls in Purgatory, and in keeping with my devotion to the Blessed Virgin Mary, I cede and renounce in favor of those holy souls all the satisfactory part of my works, and all the suffrages which may be given to me after my death, consigning them entirely into the hands of the most Blessed Virgin Mary, that she may apply them according to her good pleasure to those souls of the faithful departed whom she desires to deliver from their sufferings. Deign, O my God, to accept and bless this offering which I make to You at this moment. Amen.

Prayer for Poor Sinners

O Most Holy Trinity, Father, Son and Holy Spirit, I adore You profoundly. I offer You the Most Precious Body, Blood, Soul and Divinity of Jesus Christ, present in all the tabernacles of the world, in reparation for the outrages, sacrileges and indifference by which He is offended. By the infinite merits of the Sacred Heart of Jesus and the Immaculate Heart of Mary, I beg the conversion of poor sinners. Amen.

Eucharistic Prayer

Most Holy Trinity, I adore You! My Lord, my God, I love You in the Most Blessed Sacrament. Amen.

Rosary Decade Prayer

O my Jesus, forgive us our sins, save us from the fires of hell, lead all souls to heaven, especially those in most need of Your mercy. Amen.

Jesus, Mary and Joseph, I love you, save souls. Amen.

Prayer for Pardon

My God, I believe, I adore, I trust and I love You! I beg pardon for those who do not believe, do not adore, do not trust and do not love You. Amen.

Sacrifice Prayer

O my Jesus, I do all for love of You, in reparation for the offenses committed against the Immaculate Heart of Mary, and for the conversion of poor sinners. Amen.

Prayer for Mercy

Behold, O my God, the traitor who has so often rebelled against You. Alas! I am filled with regret; I abhor and detest with all my heart my innumerable sins. I offer You in expiation the same satisfaction which Jesus Christ offers on the altar; His merits, His blood, and Himself, God Incarnate, Who, as Victim, deigns to renew His Sacrifice daily on our altars for our sake. As my Jesus is Himself my Mediator and Advocate on the altar, and is asking You to have mercy on me through His Precious Blood, I join my voice to His adorable pleading, and ask Your forgiveness for the enormity of my sins. O

God of my heart, if my tears do not touch You, listen to the groaning of Jesus, and as He obtained mercy on the Cross for the whole world, may He obtain it for me on the altar! I humbly trust that through the merits of His Precious Blood You will forgive me all my sins, which I shall bewail to my last breath. My beloved Jesus, give me the tears of St. Peter, the contrition of Mary Magdalen, and the sorrow of all the Saints, who from sinners became true penitents, that I may obtain complete forgiveness of my sins through the Holy Sacrifice of the Mass. Amen.

Prayer to our Blessed Mother

O Mary, O Mother, most afflicted of all mothers! I feel deeply the suffering of your Immaculate Heart, most especially when you beheld your Jesus surrender Himself on the Cross, open His mouth, and expire; and, for love of this your Son, Who died for my salvation, I beseech you to recommend unto Him my soul. And do You, my Jesus, for the sake of the merits of Mary's sorrows, have mercy upon me, and grant me the grace of dying for You, as You died for me: At that hour help me to say unto You, with St. Francis of Assisi: "May I die, O my Lord, for love of the love of You, Who has vouchsafed to die for love of the love of me." Amen.

The Fifteen Prayers as revealed by Our Lord to Saint Bridget

1st Prayer—Our Father, Hail Mary...

O Jesus Christ! Eternal sweetness to those who love You, joy surpassing all joy and all desire, salvation and hope of all sinners; You who proved that You have no greater desire than to be among us even assuming our human nature during the course of time for love of us, recall all the sufferings that You endured from the first moment of Your conception, and especially during Your Passion, as it was decreed and ordained from all eternity in the Divine plan.

Remember, Lord, that during the Last Supper with Your disciples, having washed their feet, You gave them Your Precious Body and Blood, and while at the same time You sweetly consoled them, You foretold Your coming Passion.

Remember the sadness and bitterness which You experienced in Your soul as You prayed: "My soul is sorrowful even unto death."

Remember all the fear, anguish and pain that You suffered in Your delicate Body before the crucifixion, when, after having prayed three separate times, bathed in a "sweat of blood," You were betrayed by Judas, Your disciple, arrested by the people of a nation You had chosen and elevated, accused by false witnesses, unjustly judged by three judges, all this in the flower of Your youth and during the solemn Paschal season. Remember that You were despoiled of Your garments and clothed with the garments of derision; that Your face and eyes were veiled, that You were buffeted, crowned with thorns, a scepter placed in Your hands, that You were fastened to a column and crushed with blows and overwhelmed with affronts and outrages.

In memory of all these pains and sufferings which You endured before Your Passion on the Cross, grant that before I die, I may with true contrition make a sincere and entire confession, make worthy satisfaction and be granted the remission of all my sins. Amen.

2nd Prayer—Our Father, Hail Mary...

O Jesus! True Liberty of angels, Paradise of delights, remember the horror and sadness which You endured when Your enemies, like furious lions, surrounded You, and by thousands of blows, insults, lacerations, and other unheard of cruelties, tormented You at will.

Through these torments and insulting words, I beg of You, O my Savior, to deliver me from all enemies, both visible and invisible, that under Your protection, I may attain the perfection of eternal salvation. Amen.

3rd Prayer—Our Father, Hail Mary...

O Jesus! Creator of heaven and earth, Whom nothing can encompass nor limit, You enfold and hold all under Your loving power, remember the very bitter pain which You suffered when blow by blow and with hatred the Jews nailed Your sacred hands and feet to the Cross, with big blunt nails, and not finding You in a pitiable enough state to satisfy their rage, they enlarged Your wounds, and added pain to pain, and with indescribable cruelty stretched Your Body on the Cross, and dislocated Your bones by pulling them on all sides.

I beg of You, O Jesus, by the memory of this most holy and most loving suffering of the Cross, to grant me the grace to love You always as I ought. Amen.

4th Prayer—Our Father, Hail Mary...

O Jesus! Heavenly Physician raised aloft on the Cross in order that through Your wounds, ours might be healed; remember the bruises which You suffered and the weakness of all Your members which were stretched to such a degree that never was there pain like unto Your own; from the crown of Your head to the soles of Your feet there was not one spot of Your Body that was not in torment; and yet, forgetting all Your sufferings, You did not cease to pray to Your Heavenly Father for Your enemies, saying: "Father, forgive them, they know not what they do."

Through this great mercy, and in memory of this suffering, grant that the remembrance of Your most bitter Passion may effect in us a perfect contrition and the remission of all our sins. Amen.

5th Prayer—Our Father, Hail Mary...

O Jesus! Mirror of eternal splendor, remember the sadness which You experienced, when, contemplating in the light of Your Divinity the predestination of those who would be saved by the merits of Your Sacred Passion, You saw at the same time the great multitude of reprobates who would be damned for their sins, and You complained bitterly of those hopeless, lost and unfortunate sinners.

Through this abyss of compassion and pity, and especially through the goodness which You displayed to the good thief when You said to him: "This day you shall be with Me in Paradise." I beg of You, O sweet Jesus, that at the hour of my death You will show me mercy. Amen.

6th Prayer—Our Father, Hail Mary...

O Jesus! King most loving and most desirable, remember the grief which You suffered, when naked and like a common criminal, You were raised and fastened to the Cross, when all Your relatives and friends abandoned You, except Your beloved Mother who remained close to You during Your agony and whom You entrusted to Your faithful disciple when You said to Mary: "Woman, behold your son," and to St. John: "Behold your Mother."

I beg of You, O my Savior, by the sword of sorrow which pierced the soul of Your holy Mother, to have compassion on me in all my afflictions and tribulations, both corporal and spiritual and to assist me in all my trials, and especially at the hour of my death. Amen.

7th Prayer—Our Father, Hail Mary...

O Jesus! Inexhaustible fountain of compassion, Who by a profound gesture of love, said from the Cross: "I thirst!" suffered from the thirst for the salvation of the human race, I beg of You, O my Savior, to inflame in our hearts the desire to tend toward perfection in all of our acts; and to extinguish in us the concupiscence of the flesh and the ardor of worldly desires. Amen.

8th Prayer—Our Father, Hail Mary...

O Jesus! Sweetness of hearts, delight of the spirit, by the bitterness of the gall and vinegar which You tasted on the Cross for love of us, grant us the grace to receive worthily Your Precious Body and Blood during our life and at the hour of our death, that it may serve us as a remedy and consolation for our souls. Amen.

9th Prayer—Our Father, Hail Mary...

O Jesus! Royal Virtue and mental delight, recall the anguish and pain which You endured, when, from the bitterness of agonizing death and the insults of Your persecutors, You exclaimed in a loud voice that You had been forsaken by the Father, saying: "My God, My God, why have You forsaken Me?"

Through this anguish, I beg of You, O my Savior, not to abandon me during the anguish and pains of my death. Amen.

10th Prayer—Our Father, Hail Mary...

O Jesus! You Who are the beginning and the end of all things, life and virtue, remember that for our sakes You were plunged into an abyss of suffering from the soles of Your feet to the crown of Your head. In consideration of the enormity of Your wounds, teach me to keep, through pure love, Your commandments, Whose way is wide and easy for those who love You. Amen.

11th Prayer—Our Father, Hail Mary...

O Jesus! Deep abyss of mercy, I beg of You, in memory of Your wounds which penetrated to the very marrow of Your bones and to the depth of Your being, to draw me, a miserable sinner, overwhelmed by my offenses, away from sin and to hide me from Your face, justly irritated against me. Hide me in Your wounds until Your anger and indignation shall have passed away. Amen.

12th Prayer—Our Father, Hail Mary...

O Jesus! Mirror of Truth, symbol of unity, bond of charity, remember the multitude of wounds with which You were afflicted from head to foot, torn and reddened by the spilling of Your adorable Blood. O great and universal pain, which You suffered in Your virginal flesh for love of us! Sweetest Jesus! What is there that You could have done for us which You have not done!

May the fruit of Your suffering be renewed in my soul by the faithful remembrance of Your Passion, and may Your love increase in my heart each day, until I see You in eternity; You Who are the treasure of every real good and every joy, which I beg You to grant me, O Sweetest Jesus, in heaven. Amen.

13th Prayer—Our Father, Hail Mary...

O Jesus! Strong Lion, Immortal and Invincible King, remember the pain which You endured when all Your strength, moral and physical, was entirely exhausted. You bowed Your head saying: "All is consummated!"

Through this anguish and grief, I beg of You, O Lord, to have mercy on me at the hour of my death, when my mind will be greatly troubled and my soul will be in anguish. Amen.

14th Prayer—Our Father, Hail Mary...

O Jesus! Only-Begotten Son of the Father, Splendor and Figure of His Substance, remember the simple and humble recommendation You made of Your soul to the Eternal Father, saying: "Father, into Your hands I commend My Spirit"; and when Your Body, all torn, and Your Heart, broken, and the bowels of Your mercy open to redeem us, You expired. Through this precious death, I beg You, O King of Saints, comfort me and give me help to resist the devil, the flesh, and the world so that, being dead to the world, I may live for You alone. I beg of You at the hour of my death to receive me, a pilgrim and an exile returning to You. Amen.

15th Prayer—Our Father, Hail Mary...

O Jesus! True and fruitful Vine! Remember the abundant outpouring of Blood which You so generously shed from Your Sacred Body as juice from grapes in a wine press.

From Your side, pierced with the lance by a soldier, Blood and water issued forth until there was not left in Your Body a single drop, and finally, like a bundle of myrrh lifted to the very top of the Cross, Your delicate flesh was destroyed, the very substance of Your Body withered, and the marrow of Your bones dried up.

Through this bitter Passion and through the outpouring of Your Precious Blood, I beg of You, O Sweet Jesus, to receive my soul when I am in my death agony. Amen.

O Sweet Jesus! Pierce my heart so that my tears of penitence and love will be my bread day and night; may I be converted entirely to You; may my heart be Your perpetual habitation, may my conversation be pleasing to You, and may the end of my life be so praiseworthy that I may merit heaven, and there, with Your saints, praise You forever and ever. Amen.

Our Father, Hail Mary, Glory be (3 times)

Salutation of the Wound in the Shoulder of Jesus

O most loving Jesus, meekest Lamb of God, I, N., a miserable sinner, salute and worship the most Sacred Wound of Your Shoulder on which You bore Your heavy Cross, which so tore Your flesh and laid bare Your bones as to inflict on You an anguish greater than any other wound of Your most Blessed Body. I adore You, O Jesus most sorrowful. I praise

You, I bless You, I glorify You and give You thanks for this most sacred and most painful Wound. I beseech You by that exceeding pain, and the crushing burden of Your heavy Cross, to be merciful to me, a sinner, to forgive me all my mortal and venial sins, and to lead me on towards Heaven along the way of the Cross. Amen.

Invocation in honor of the Holy Wounds of Our Lord Jesus Christ

On the large beads:

Eternal Father, I offer You the Wounds of Our Lord Jesus Christ to heal the wounds of our souls. Amen

On the small beads:

My Jesus, grant me pardon and mercy through the merits of Your Sacred Wounds. Amen.

Prayer to Jesus Crucified

Look down upon me, good and gentle Jesus, while before Your face I humbly kneel, and with the most fervent desire of my soul pray and beseech You to fix deep in my heart lively sentiments of faith, hope, and charity, true contrition for my sins, and a firm purpose of amendment, while with deep affection and grief of soul, I contemplate and ponder over Your five most precious wounds, calling to mind the words of the prophet David concerning You, O good Jesus: "They have pierced my hands and my feet; they have numbered all my bones." Amen.

Anima Christi

Soul of Christ, sanctify me.
Body of Christ, save me.
Blood of Christ, inebriate me.
Water from the side of Christ, wash me.
Passion of Christ, strengthen me.
O good Jesus, hear me.
Within Your Wounds hide me.
Never permit me to be separated from You.
From the malicious enemy defend me.
In the hour of my death call me,
And bid me come to You,
That with Your saints, I may praise You
Forever and ever. Amen.

To Our Lord on the Cross

My Crucified Jesus, mercifully accept the prayer which I now make to You for help in the moment of my death, when at its approach, all my senses shall fail me. When, therefore, O sweetest Jesus, my weary and downcast eyes can no longer look up to You, be mindful of the loving gaze which I now turn on You, and have mercy on me. When my parched lips can no longer kiss Your most sacred wounds, remember then those kisses which now I imprint on You, and have mercy on me. When my cold hands can no longer embrace Your Cross, forget not the affection with which I embrace it now, and have mercy on me. And when at length, my swollen and lifeless tongue can no longer speak, remember that I called upon You now.

Jesus, Mary and Joseph, I give you my heart, my soul and my life; Jesus, Mary and Joseph, assist me in my last agony; Jesus, Mary and Joseph, may I breathe forth my soul in peace with you. Amen.

Act of Consecration to the Sacred Heart of Jesus

O amiable Heart of my Savior, I adore You!
O gracious Heart of my Jesus, I love You!
O compassionate Heart, I give You my heart, and am deeply moved by all You have done and suffered for me.

Yes, I give You my whole heart; attach it

eternally to Yourself, inflame it with Your love, inspire it with Your sentiments, make it know Your Will and practice Your virtues. Amen.

Veni, Creator

Come, O Creator Spirit Blest!
And in our souls take up Your rest;
Come with Your grace and heavenly aid,
To fill the hearts which You have made.
Great Paraclete! To You we cry,
O highest gift of God most high!
O font of life! O fire of love!
And sweet anointing from above.
You in Your sevenfold gifts are known,
The finger of God's hand we own;
The promise of the Father, Thou!
Who do the tongue with power endow.
Kindle our senses from above,
And make our hearts o'erflow with love;
With patience firm and virtue high
The weakness of our flesh supply.
Far from us drive the foe we dread,
And grant us Your true peace instead;
So shall we not, with You for guide,
Turn from the path of life aside.
Oh, may Your grace on us bestow

The Father and the Son to know,
And You through endless times confessed
Of both the eternal Spirit blest.
All glory while the ages run
Be to the Father and the Son
Who rose from death; the same to Thee,
O Holy Spirit, eternally. Amen.

Magnificat

My soul proclaims the greatness of the Lord;
    my spirit rejoices in God my Savior
    for He has looked upon His lowly servant .
From this day all generations will call me blessed:
    the Almighty has done great things for me,
    and holy is His name.
He has mercy on those who fear Him
    in every generation.
He has shown the strength of His arm,
    and has scattered the proud in their conceit.
He has cast down the mighty from their thrones,
    and has lifted up the lowly.
He has filled the hungry with good things,
    and the rich He has sent away empty.
He has come to the help of His servant Israel
    for He has remembered His promise of
    mercy,

the promise He made to our fathers,
to Abraham and his children forever. Amen.
Glory be to the Father, etc.

Ave, Maris Stella

Hail, bright star of ocean,
God's own Mother blest,
Ever sinless Virgin,
Gate of heavenly rest.
Taking that sweet Ave
Which from Gabriel came,
Peace confirm within us,
Changing Eva's name.

Break the captives' fetters,
Light on blindness pour,
All our ills expelling,
Every bliss implore.

Show thyself a Mother;
May the Word Divine,
Born for us thy Infant,
Hear our prayers through thine.

Virgin all excelling,
Mildest of the mild,

Freed from guilt, preserve us,
Pure and undefiled.

Keep our life all spotless,
Make our way secure,
Till we find in Jesus
Joy forevermore.

Through the highest Heaven
To the Almighty Three,
Father, Son and Spirit,
One same glory be. Amen.

Litany of the Holy Spirit

Lord, have mercy on us.
Christ, have mercy on us.
Lord, have mercy on us.
Father all powerful, *have mercy on us.*
Jesus, Eternal Son of the Father, Redeemer of the world, *save us.*
Spirit of the Father and the Son, boundless life of both, *sanctify us.*
Holy Trinity, *hear us.*
Holy Spirit, Who proceeds from the Father and the Son, *enter our hearts.*
Holy Spirit, Who are equal to the Father and

the Son, *enter our hearts.*
Promise of God the Father,
Ray of heavenly light,
Author of all good,
Source of heavenly water,
Consuming fire,
Ardent charity,
Spiritual unction,
Spirit of love and truth,
Spirit of wisdom and understanding,
Spirit of counsel and fortitude,
Spirit of knowledge and piety,
Spirit of the fear of the Lord,
Spirit of grace and prayer,
Spirit of peace and meekness,
Spirit of modesty and innocence,
Holy Spirit, the Comforter,
Holy Spirit, the Sanctifier,
Holy Spirit, Who governs the Church,
Gift of God, the Most High,
Spirit Who fills the universe,
Spirit of the adoption of the children of God,

have mercy on us.

Holy Spirit, *inspire us with horror of sin.*
Holy Spirit, *come and renew the face of the earth.*
Holy Spirit, *shed Your light in our souls.*
Holy Spirit, *engrave Your law in our hearts.*

Holy Spirit, *inflame us with the flame of Your love.*
Holy Spirit, *open to us the treasures of Your graces.*
Holy Spirit, *teach us to pray well.*
Holy Spirit, *enlighten us with Your heavenly inspirations.*
Holy Spirit, *lead us in the way of salvation.*
Holy Spirit, *grant us the only necessary knowledge.*
Holy Spirit, *inspire in us the practice of good.*
Holy Spirit, *grant us the merits of all virtues.*
Holy Spirit, *make us persevere in justice.*
Holy Spirit, *be our everlasting reward.*
Lamb of God, Who takes away the sins of the world, *send us Your Holy Spirit.*
Lamb of God, Who takes away the sins of the world, *pour down into our souls the gifts of the Holy Spirit.*
Lamb of God, Who takes away the sins of the world, *grant us the Spirit of wisdom and piety.*

V. Come, Holy Spirit! Fill the hearts of the faithful.

R. And enkindle in them the fire of Your love.

Let us Pray

Grant, O merciful Father, that Your Divine Spirit may enlighten, inflame and purify us, that He may penetrate us with His heavenly dew and make us fruitful in good works; through our Lord Jesus Christ, Your Son, Who with You, in the unity of the same Spirit, lives and reigns forever and ever. Amen.

Litany of the Blessed Virgin

Lord, have mercy on us.
Christ, have mercy on us.
Lord, have mercy on us.
Christ, hear us.
Christ, graciously hear us.
God the Father of heaven, *have mercy on us.*
God the Son, Redeemer of the world, *have mercy on us.*
God the Holy Spirit, *have mercy on us.*
Holy Trinity, one God, *have mercy on us.*
Holy Mary,
Holy Mother of God,
Holy Virgin of virgins,
Mother of Christ,
Mother of divine grace,
Mother most pure,
Mother most chaste, *pray for us.*

Mother inviolate,
Mother undefiled,
Mother most amiable,
Mother most admirable,
Mother of good counsel,
Mother of our Creator,
Mother of our Savior,
Mother of the Church,
Virgin most prudent,
Virgin most venerable,
Virgin most renowned,
Virgin most powerful,
Virgin most merciful,
Virgin most faithful,
Mirror of justice,
Seat of wisdom,
Cause of our joy,
Spiritual vessel,
Vessel of honor,
Singular vessel of devotion,
Mystical rose,
Tower of David,
Tower of ivory,
House of gold,
Ark of the covenant,
Gate of Heaven,
Morning star,

pray for us.

Health of the sick,
Refuge of sinners,
Comforter of the afflicted,
Help of Christians,
Queen of angels,
Queen of patriarchs,
Queen of prophets,
Queen of Apostles,
Queen of martyrs,
Queen of confessors,
Queen of virgins,
Queen of all saints,
Queen conceived without original sin,
Queen of the most holy Rosary,
Queen assumed into Heaven,
Queen of peace,

pray for us.

Lamb of God, Who takes away the sins of the world, *spare us, O Lord.*
Lamb of God, Who takes away the sins of the world, *graciously hear us, O Lord.*
Lamb of God, Who takes away the sins of the world, *have mercy on us.*
Christ hear us,
Christ graciously hear us.

V. Pray for us, O holy Mother of God.
R. That we may be made worthy of the promises of Christ.

Let us Pray

Grant unto us, Your servants, we beseech You, O Lord God, at all times to enjoy health of soul and body; and by the glorious intercession of the Blessed Mary, ever virgin, when freed from the sorrows of this present life, to enter into that joy which has no end. Through Christ our Lord. Amen.

Litany of the Holy Name of Jesus

Lord, have mercy on us.
Christ, have mercy on us.
Lord, have mercy on us.
Jesus, hear us.
Jesus, graciously hear us.
God the Father of heaven,
God the Son, Redeemer of the world,
God the Holy Spirit,
Holy Trinity, one God,
Jesus, Son of the living God,
Jesus, splendor of the Father,
Jesus, brightness of eternal light,
Jesus, King of glory,
Jesus, sun of justice,
Jesus, Son of the Virgin Mary,
Jesus, most amiable,
Jesus, most admirable,

have mercy on us.

Jesus, mighty God,
Jesus, Father of the world to come,
Jesus, angel of the great council,
Jesus, most powerful,
Jesus, most patient,
Jesus, most obedient,
Jesus, meek and humble of heart,
Jesus, lover of chastity,
Jesus, lover of us,
Jesus, God of peace,
Jesus, author of life,
Jesus, model of virtues,
Jesus, lover of souls,
Jesus, our God,
Jesus, our refuge,
Jesus, Father of the poor,
Jesus, treasure of the faithful,
Jesus, Good Shepherd,
Jesus, true light,
Jesus, eternal wisdom,
Jesus, infinite goodness,
Jesus, our way, our truth and our life,
Jesus, joy of angels,
Jesus, King of patriarchs,
Jesus, master of Apostles,
Jesus, teacher of Evangelists,
Jesus, strength of martyrs,

have mercy on us.

Jesus, light of confessors,
Jesus, purity of virgins,
Jesus, crown of all saints,
Be merciful, *spare us, O Jesus.*
Be merciful, *graciously hear us, O Jesus.*
From all evil,
From all sin,
From Your wrath,
From the snares of the devil,
From the spirit of fornication,
From everlasting death,
From the neglect of Your inspirations,
Through the mystery of Your holy Incarnation,
Through Your nativity,
Through Your infancy,
Through Your most divine life,
Through Your labors,
Through Your agony and Passion,
Through Your cross and dereliction,
Through Your sufferings,
Through Your death and burial,
Through Your Resurrection,
Through Your Ascension,
Through Your institution of the most Holy Eucharist,
Through Your joys,
Through Your glory,

have mercy on us.

Jesus, deliver us.

Lamb of God, Who takes away the sins of the world, *spare us, O Jesus.*
Lamb of God, Who takes away the sins of the world, *graciously hear us, O Jesus.*
Lamb of God, Who takes away the sins of the world, *have mercy on us.*
Jesus hear us,
Jesus, graciously hear us.

Let us Pray

O Lord, Jesus Christ, Who said: Ask and you shall receive; seek and you shall find; knock and it shall be opened unto you: grant, we beseech You, to us who ask the gift of Your divine love, that we may ever love You with all our hearts, and in all our words and actions, and never cease praising You.

Give us, O Lord, a perpetual fear and love of Your holy Name; for You never fail to govern those whom You solidly establish in Your love. Who lives and reigns world without end. Amen.

Litany of the Sacred Heart of Jesus

Lord, have mercy on us.
Christ, have mercy on us.
Lord, have mercy on us.
Christ, hear us.
Christ, graciously hear us.

God the Father of Heaven,
God the Son, Redeemer of the world,
God the Holy Spirit,
Holy Trinity, one God,
Heart of Jesus, Son of the Eternal Father,
Heart of Jesus, formed by the Holy Spirit in the womb of the Virgin Mother,
Heart of Jesus, substantially united with the Word of God,
Heart of Jesus, of infinite majesty,
Heart of Jesus, holy temple of God,
Heart of Jesus, house of God and gate of Heaven,
Heart of Jesus, burning furnace of charity,
Heart of Jesus, abode of justice and love,
Heart of Jesus, full of goodness and love,
Heart of Jesus, abyss of all virtues,
Heart of Jesus, most worthy of all praise,
Heart of Jesus, King and center of all hearts,
Heart of Jesus, in whom are all the treasures of wisdom and knowledge,
Heart of Jesus, in whom dwells all the fullness of divinity,
Heart of Jesus, in whom the Father was well pleased,
Heart of Jesus, of whose fullness we have all received,

have mercy on us.

Heart of Jesus, desire of the everlasting hills,
Heart of Jesus, patient and most merciful,
Heart of Jesus, enriching all who invoke You,
Heart of Jesus, fountain of life and holiness,
Heart of Jesus, propitiation for our sins,
Heart of Jesus, loaded down with opprobrium,
Heart of Jesus, bruised for our offenses,
Heart of Jesus, obedient unto death,
Heart of Jesus, pierced with a lance,
Heart of Jesus, source of all consolation,
Heart of Jesus, our life and resurrection,
Heart of Jesus, our peace and reconciliation,
Heart of Jesus, victim for sin,
Heart of Jesus, salvation of those who trust in You,
Heart of Jesus, delight of all the saints,
Lamb of God, Who takes away the sins of the world, *spare us, O Lord.*
Lamb of God, Who takes away the sins of the world, *graciously hear us, O Lord.*
Lamb of God, Who takes away the sins of the world, *have mercy on us.*

have mercy on us.

V. Jesus meek and humble of heart.
R. Make our hearts like unto Thine.

Let us Pray

Almighty and everlasting God, graciously regard the heart of Your highly beloved Son and the acts of praise and satisfaction which He renders to You on behalf of us sinners, and through their merit grant pardon to us who implore Your mercy, in the name of Your Son Jesus Christ, Who lives and reigns with You in the unity of the Holy Spirit, one God world without end. Amen.

Litany of Saint Joseph

Lord, have mercy on us.
Christ, have mercy on us.
Lord, have mercy on us.
Christ, hear us.
Christ, graciously hear us.
God the Father of Heaven, *have mercy on us.*
God the Son, Redeemer of the world, *have mercy on us.*
God the Holy Spirit, *have mercy on us.*
Holy Trinity, one God, *have mercy on us.*
Holy Mary, *pray for us.*
Saint Joseph,
Illustrious Son of David,
Light of the Patriarchs,
Spouse of the Mother of God,

pray for us.

Chaste Guardian of the Virgin,
Foster-Father of the Son of God,
Watchful Defender of Christ,
Head of the Holy Family,
Joseph most just,
Joseph most chaste,
Joseph most prudent,
Joseph most valiant,
Joseph most obedient,
Joseph most faithful,
Mirror of patience,
Lover of poverty,
Model of workmen,
Glory of domestic life,
Guardian of virgins,
Pillar of families,
Solace of the afflicted,
Hope of the sick,
Patron of the dying,
Terror of demons,
Protector of Holy Church.

pray for us.

Lamb of God, Who takes away the sins of the world, *spare us, O Lord.*
Lamb of God, Who takes away the sins of the world, *graciously hear us, O Lord.*
Lamb of God, Who takes away the sins of the world, *have mercy on us.*

V. He made him the lord of His house.
R. And the ruler of all His possessions.

Let us Pray

O God, Who in Your unspeakable providence chose Saint Joseph to be the spouse of Your most Holy Mother, grant that as we venerate him as our protector on earth, we may deserve to have him as our intercessor in Heaven through our Lord Jesus Christ, Your Son. Amen.

Prayer to Saint Joseph

To you, Saint Joseph, we come with confidence in this hour of need, trusting in your powerful protection. Your loving service to the Immaculate Virgin Mother of God and your fatherly affection for the Child Jesus inspire us with faith in the power of your intercession before the throne of God.

We pray, first of all, for the Church: that it may be free from error and corruption, and be a shining light of universal love and justice.

We ask your intercession for our loved ones in their trials and adversities, that they may be inspired by the love, obedience and affection of the Holy Family, and be to each other a mutual source of consolation and Christian fidelity.

We ask your intercession also for our special need (here mention the grace desired).

Keep us one and all under your protection so that, strengthened by your example and assistance, we may lead a holy life, die a happy death, and come to the possession of everlasting happiness in heaven. Amen.

Let us Pray

Assist us, Lord, by the merits of Your foster father, Saint Joseph, spouse of Your most Holy Mother. May his help gain for us what our own efforts cannot obtain. This we ask through You Who live and reign with God the Father in the union of the Holy Spirit, one God, for all the ages. Amen.

Saint Joseph, Patron of Workers

Blessed Saint Joseph, patron of all working people, obtain for me the grace to labor in a spirit of penance for the atonement of my many sins. Help me to be conscientious in my work so that I may give as full a measure as I have received.

May I labor in a spirit of thankfulness and joy, ever mindful of all the gifts I have received from God that enable me to perform these tasks. Permit me to work in peace, patience and moderation, keeping in mind the account I must one day give of time lost, talents unused, good omitted and vanity of success, so fatal to the work of God. Glorious Saint Joseph, may my labors be all for Jesus, all through Mary and all after your holy example in life and in death. Amen.

Saint Joseph, Chaste Spouse of Mary

O Holy Joseph, chaste spouse of the Mother of God, most glorious advocate of all who are in danger or in their last agony, and most faithful protector of all the servants of Mary, I N., in the presence of Jesus and Mary, do from this moment choose you for my powerful patron and advocate, and I implore you to obtain for me through your powerful intercession the grace of a happy death.

Receive me, therefore, for your perpetual servant, and recommend me to the constant protection of Mary, your spouse, and to the everlasting mercies of Jesus my Savior.

Assist me in all the actions of my life, which I now offer to the greater glory of Jesus and Mary.

Never, therefore, forsake me; and whatsoever grace you see most necessary and profitable for me, obtain it for me now and also at the hour of my death.

Through your gracious intercession may there be granted me in my last hour all the graces I need, through the merits of Jesus Christ, my Savior, Who together with the Father and the Holy Spirit, lives and reigns, world without end. Amen.

Prayer for Virginity

O Blessed Saint Joseph, faithful guardian and protector of virgins, to whom God entrusted Jesus and Mary, I implore you by the love which you did bear them, to preserve me from every defilement of soul and body, that I may always serve them in holiness and purity of love. Amen.

Prayer for Purity

Saint Joseph, father and guardian of virgins, into whose faithful keeping were entrusted Innocence itself, I pray and beseech you through Jesus and Mary, those pledges so dear to you, to keep me from all uncleanness, and to grant that my mind may be untainted, my heart pure, and my body chaste. Help me always to serve Jesus and Mary in perfect chastity. Amen.

For A Happy Death

O Blessed Saint Joseph, who died in the arms of Jesus and Mary, obtain for me, I beseech you, the grace of a happy death. In that hour of dread and anguish, assist me by your power against the enemies of my salvation. Into your hands, living and dying, Jesus, Mary and Joseph, I commend my soul. Amen.

O Jesus, Living in Mary

O Jesus, living in Mary,
Come and live in Your servants,
In the spirit of Your holiness,
In the fullness of Your might,
In the truth of Your virtues,
In the perfection of Your ways,
In the communion of Your mysteries,
Subdue every hostile power
In Your Spirit, for the glory of the Father.
    Amen.

Prayers from The Little Office of the Immaculate Conception of the Blessed Virgin Mary

Come, my lips, and wide proclaim,
The Blessed Virgin's spotless fame.

V. O Lady, make haste to befriend me.
R. From the hands of the enemy mightily defend me.

Glory be to the Father, and to the Son, and to the Holy Spirit.
As it was in the beginning, is now, and ever shall be, world without end. Amen. Alleluia.

Hymn

Hail, Mistress of earth!
Hail, Virgin most pure,
Of Immaculate birth!
Clear Star of the morning,
In beauty enshrined!
O Lady, make speed
To the help of mankind.
Thee God in the depth
Of eternity chose;
And formed thee all fair
As His glorious Spouse;

And called thee His Word's
Own Mother to be,
By Whom He created
The earth, sky, and sea.

V. God elected her, and pre-elected her.
R. He made her to dwell in His tabernacle.

Let us Pray

O Holy Mary, Queen of Heaven, Mother of our Lord Jesus Christ, and Mistress of the world, who forsakes no one, and despises no one; look upon me, O Lady, with an eye of pity, and entreat for me, of your beloved Son, the forgiveness of all my sins; that, as I now celebrate with devout affection, your holy and Immaculate Conception (and glorious Assumption and Coronation in Heaven), so hereafter, I may receive the prize of eternal blessedness by the grace of Him, Whom you, in virginity brought forth, Jesus Christ our Lord, Who with the Father and the Holy Spirit, lives and reigns in perfect Trinity, God, world without end. Amen.

V. O Lady, hear my prayer.
R. And let my cry come unto you.

V. Let us bless the Lord.
R Thanks be to God.

May the souls of the faithful departed through the mercy of God rest in peace. Amen.

V. O Lady, make haste to befriend me.
R. From the hands of the enemy mightily defend me.

Glory be to the Father, etc. Alleluia.

Hymn

Hail, Virgin most wise!
Hail Deity's shrine!
With seven fair pillars
And table divine!
Preserved from the guilt
Which has come on us all!
Exempt, in the womb,
From the taint of the fall.
O new star of Jacob!
Of Angels, the Queen!
O gate of the Saints!
O Mother of men.
O terrible as
An embattled array
Be now of the faithful
Their refuge and stay.

V. The Lord Himself created her in the Holy Spirit.
R. And poured her out among all His Works.

V. O Lady, hear my prayer.
R. And let my cry come unto you.

Let us pray: O Holy Mary, Queen of, etc.

V. O Lady, hear my prayer.
R. And let my cry come unto you.

V. Let us bless the Lord.
R. Thanks be to God.

May the souls of the faithful departed through the mercy of God rest in peace. Amen.

V. O Lady, make haste to befriend me.
R. From the hands of the enemy mightily defend me.

Glory be to the Father, etc. Alleluia.

Hymn

Hail, Solomon's throne!
Pure ark of the law!
Fair rainbow! and bush
Which the Patriarch saw.
Hail, Gideon's fleece!
Hail blossoming rod!
Samson's sweet honeycomb!
Portal of God!
Well fitting it was,

That a Son so divine
Should preserve from all touch
Of original sin.
Nor suffer by smallest
Defect to be stained,
That Mother, whom He
For Himself, had ordained.

V. O Lady, make haste to befriend me.
R. And my throne is on the pillar of the clouds.

V. O Lady, hear my prayer.
R. And let my cry come unto you.

Let us pray: O Holy Mary, Queen of, etc.

V. O Lady, hear my prayer.
R. And let my cry come unto you.

V. Let us bless the Lord.
R. Thanks be to God.

May the souls of the faithful departed through the mercy of God rest in peace. Amen.

V. O Lady, make haste to befriend me.
R. From the hands of the enemy mightily defend me.

Glory be to the Father, etc. Alleluia.

Hymn

Hail, Virginal Mother!
Hail, purity's cell!
Fair shrine where the Trinity
Loveth to dwell.
Hail, garden of pleasure!
Celestial balm!
Cedar of chastity.
Martyrdom's palm!
O land set apart
From uses profane!
And free from the curse
Which in Adam began.
O city of God!
O gate of the East!
In you is all grace,
O joy of the blest!

V. As the lily among the thorns.
R. So is my beloved among the daughters of Adam.

V. O Lady, hear my prayer.
R. And let my cry come unto you.

Let us pray: O Holy Mary, Queen of, etc.

V. O Lady, hear my prayer.
R. And let my cry come unto you.

V. Let us bless the Lord.
R. Thanks be to God.

May the souls of the faithful departed through the mercy of God rest in peace. Amen.

V. O Lady, make haste to befriend me.
R. From the hands of the enemy mightily defend me.

Hymn

Hail city of refuge!
Hail, David's high tower!
With battlements crowned
And girded with power!
Filled at your conception
With love and with light!
The dragon by you
Was shorn of his might.
O Woman most valiant!
O Judith, thrice blessed!
As David was nursed
At his fair mother's breast.
As the savior of Egypt
Upon Rachel's knee,
So the world's great Redeemer,
Was cherished by thee.

V. You are all fair, my beloved.
R. And the original stain was never in you.

V. O Lady, hear my prayer.
R. And let my cry come unto you.

Let us pray: O Holy Mary, Queen of, etc.

V. O Lady, hear my prayer.
R. And let my cry come unto you.

V. Let us bless the Lord.
R. Thanks be to God.

May the souls of the faithful departed through the mercy of God rest in peace. Amen.

V. O Lady, make haste to befriend me.
R. From the hands of the enemy mightily defend me.

Glory be to the Father, etc. Alleluia.

Hymn

Hail, dial of Achaz!
On you, the true Sun,
Told backward the course
Which from old He had run!
And, that Man might be raised
Submitting to shame,

A little more low
Than the angels became.
You, wrapt in the blaze
Of His Infinite light,
Do shine as the morn
On the confines of night.
As the moon on the lost
Through obscurity dawns;
The serpent's destroyer!
A lily 'mid thorns!

V. I made an unfailing light to arise in heaven.
R. And as a mist I overspread the whole earth.

V. O Lady, hear my prayer.
R. And let my cry come unto you.

Let us pray: O Holy Mary, Queen of, etc.

V. O Lady, hear my prayer.
R. And let my cry come unto you.

V. Let us bless the Lord.
R. Thanks be to God.

May the souls of the faithful departed through the mercy of God rest in peace. Amen.

V. May Jesus Christ, your Son, reconciled by your prayers, O Lady, convert our hearts.

R. And turn away His anger from us.

V. O Lady, make haste to befriend me.
R. From the hands of the enemy mightily defend me.

Glory be to the Father, etc. Alleluia.

Hymn

Hail, Mother most pure!
Hail Virgin renowned!
Hail, Queen with the stars
As a diadem crowned!
Above all the angels
In glory untold,
Standing next to the King
In a vesture of gold.
O Mother of mercy!
O star of the wave!
O hope of the guilty!
O light of the grave!
Through thee may we come
To the haven of rest;
And see Heaven's King
In the courts of the blest!

V. Your name, O Mary, is as oil poured out.
R. Your servants have loved you exceedingly.

V. O Lady, hear my prayer.
R. And let my cry come unto you.

Let us pray: O Holy Mary, Queen of, etc.

V. O Lady, hear my prayer.
R. And let my cry come unto you.

V. Let us bless the Lord.
R. Thanks be to God.

May the souls of the faithful departed through the mercy of God rest in peace. Amen.
The Office concludes as follows:

> These praises and prayers
> I lay at thy feet,
> O Virgin of virgins!
> O Mary most sweet!
> Be thou my true guide
> Through this pilgrimage here;
> And stand by my side
> When death draweth near.

Ant. This is the admirable Virgin who has contracted neither original sin, nor the least actual sin.

V. O Holy Virgin, conceived without sin.
R. Pray for us to God the Father whose Son you brought forth.

Let us Pray

O God, who in preserving the most Holy Virgin from the stain of original sin prepared for Your Son a worthy dwelling in the womb of this Immaculate Virgin, we beseech You, that as You preserved her from all sin by the anticipated merits of the death of this same Son, You would also vouchsafe through her intercession, to give us grace to possess You forever, purified from all our sins. Through Jesus Christ our Lord. Amen.

Say the Memorare.

The New Secret of Salvation

Fatima and The Three Little Shepherds

Among the many Apparitions of Our Lady, memorable is the mysterious event that occurred at Fatima, in Portugal, the war-year 1917. The Blessed Virgin appeared to three innocent shepherds near Cova da Iria; they were Lucy, ten years old, and her two cousins, Francesco and Jacinta Marto (both beatified by Pope John Paul II on May 13, 2000), the former nine, the latter seven years of age.

Soon the smaller ones passed to eternal life, while Lucy, a few years after the apparitions, entered the convent of St. Dorothy at Tuy in Spain, where, on the 3rd of October, 1928, she was named Sister Mary Lucy of the Sorrowful Mother.

In 1948, Sister Lucy left the Convent of the Sisters of St. Dorothy and entered a Carmelite Convent in Portugal.

The Blessed Virgin came on earth to bring a Message from her Divine Son, to warn the world of present and future evils, to entrust to us a great secret with the promise of peace if the Rosary be recited, and devotion to the Immaculate Heart of Mary be spread throughout the world.

Let us hear with gratitude and filial affection the touching and impressive words of Our Lady of Fatima.

First Apparition

Here is the first message: "I have come to ask you that you return here six times, at the same hour, the 13th of the month, and in October I shall tell you who I am and what I want from you. Offer yourselves to God, practice self-denial, accept willingly all the trials He will send to you in reparation for the sins against the Divine Majesty; do this for the conversion of sinners and also to amend for all blasphemies and offenses made to the Immaculate Heart of Mary."

Second Apparition

It was the feast of St. Anthony; the three little shepherds together with other people had gathered at the same place, and had devoutly said the Rosary, when the beautiful Lady appeared saying: "Recite the Rosary every day, and after the 'Glory' of each decade add this prayer: 'O my Jesus, forgive us our sins, save us from the fires of hell, lead all souls to heaven, especially those in most need of Your mercy.'"

Then she told Lucy: "I shall come soon to take Jacinta and Francesco with me. You will remain on earth much longer, for Jesus wishes you to establish in the world devotion to my Immaculate Heart." Then to each child she confided a secret, forbidding them, however, to reveal it to anyone.

Third Apparition — July 13th

The news of the apparition of Our Lady began to spread. On the 13th of July more than 5,000 people had gathered near Cova da Iria.

The Lady dressed in white appeared and recommended:

"Say the Rosary every day; say it frequently so that the war might end, because only the intercession of the Virgin could obtain this favor for suffering humanity. Continue to come here every month, and on the 13th of October I shall tell you who I am and what I desire. A miracle will occur so that the world will believe in my apparitions."

Apparitions of August and September

Lucy told the 30,000 people who had gathered: "You must pray." The Vision appeared, saying: "Persevere in reciting the Rosary, if you wish to see the end of the war. Pray hard and make sacrifices for the conversion of sinners. Know that many souls go to Hell because there is no one who is willing to sacrifice himself for them."

Last Apparition
The Long Expected Message

The crowd was immense: 70,000 people waiting to see what would happen. The deaf, dumb, blind and crippled were praying for a miracle to happen that would set them free from their ailments. Lo, and behold! the divine Vision appeared again, and Lucy, in order to obey the Ecclesiastical Authorities, exclaimed: "Who are you, and what do you want?" The Vision answered: "I AM THE LADY OF THE

ROSARY and ask that a shrine be erected here in my honor. I have come to plead with all the faithful to amend their lives, to beg pardon for their sins and to resolve never to offend the Lord again. Continue to say the Rosary every day. I promise that, if men will change their sinful life, I will answer their prayers, and the war will end soon."

Frightful Vision

Very rapidly, the Virgin showed the three innocent children a vision of Hell, where thousands of sinful souls fall every day. Frightened, the children looked at Mary who, with sorrowful accent, said: "In order to save sinners, the Lord wishes to establish in the world devotion to my Immaculate Heart. If what I tell you will be done, many souls will be saved, and there will be peace; but, if this is not done, Divine Justice will require new and heavier punishments. The present war (1914-1918) is about to end, but if men do not cease to offend God, in a short time, during the next Pontificate (of Pius XI) another war, worse than this, will start. (It was the Second World War.)

"When a night shall be brightened by a strange light, know that it is the sign God gives you to warn the world that the punishment for its crimes is near. There will be war, famine, and persecution against the Church and the Holy Father. In order to prevent this, I urge the consecration of the world to my Immaculate Heart, and the Communion of Reparation every first Saturday of the month.

"If what I ask is done, Russia will be converted, and there will be peace, otherwise (as sadly happened) grave errors will spread through the world and will cause more wars and persecutions against the Church; many good Christians will suffer martyrdom, and the Holy Father will suffer greatly (the assassination attempt on Pope John Paul II, May 13, 1981, is specifically referred to here according to Sr. Lucy); several nations will be destroyed, but in the end, my Immaculate Heart will be triumphant! The Holy Father will consecrate Russia to me, and humanity will have an era of peace."

Queen of the Apostles

The ROSARY

First Joyful Mystery

The Annunciation

To obtain humility

THE ROSARY

Begin the Rosary with the Apostles' Creed, the Our Father and three Hail Marys.

The Joyful Mysteries

I — The Annunciation

Was it the night wind that brushed her cheek in the singing silence as "the angel of the Lord declared unto Mary"? The girl, startled at the slight movement, looked up and through Gabriel into the will of God. Then the Son of God enfolded Himself in her heart, and "the Word was made Flesh."

Our Father, ten Hail Marys, Glory be to the Father.

Prayer Our Lady taught Jacinta to say after each decade.

O my Jesus, forgive us our sins, save us from the fires of hell, lead all souls to heaven, especially those in most need of Your mercy. Amen.

Second Joyful Mystery

The Visitation

Love of neighbor

II — The Visitation

Through the shining ecstasy of spring, Mary, impelled to share the Treasure beneath her heart, "hastened into the hill country." There her cousin Elizabeth waited, age anticipating youth, to proclaim Mary "blessed among women," and as John leapt into the saving state of grace, the Magnificat was born.

Our Father, ten Hail Marys, Glory be to the Father.

Prayer Our Lady taught Jacinta to say after each decade.

O my Jesus, forgive us our sins, save us from the fires of hell, lead all souls to heaven, especially those in most need of Your mercy. Amen.

Third Joyful Mystery

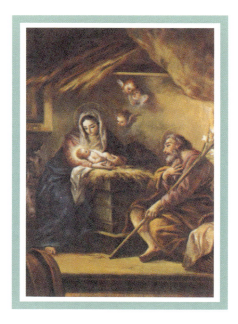

The Birth of Christ

Detachment from the world

III — The Birth of Christ

A night of dancing stars and angels' caroling, of shepherds stunned into ecstasy, of one lone light in a cattle cave, and the Babe sprang from His mother's heart into the nipping cold of a world that still rejects Him.

Our Father, ten Hail Marys, Glory be to the Father.

Prayer Our Lady taught Jacinta to say after each decade.

O my Jesus, forgive us our sins, save us from the fires of hell, lead all souls to heaven, especially those in most need of Your mercy. Amen.

Fourth Joyful Mystery

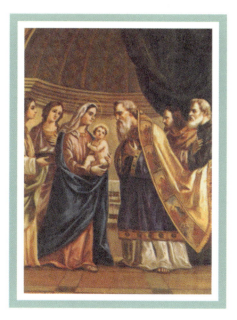

The Presentation

Respect for authority

IV — The Presentation

They ascended the steps into the Temple. The seven-branched candle swayed slightly, while the soft cooing of silver doves hid the tumult of the girl's heart.

Mary offered flesh of her lily flesh to God. Through Simeon and Anna the rumor of Him went abroad, quivering through the Holy City.

Our Father, ten Hail Marys, Glory be to the Father.

Prayer Our Lady taught Jacinta to say after each decade.

O my Jesus, forgive us our sins, save us from the fires of hell, lead all souls to heaven, especially those in most need of Your mercy. Amen.

Fifth Joyful Mystery

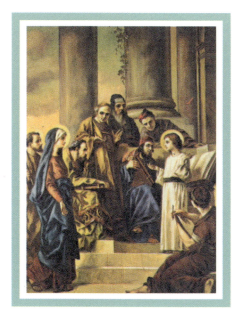

Finding the Child Jesus in the Temple

To obtain the love of Jesus

V — Finding the Child Jesus in the Temple

The dusk of the third day, dusk petalled with dew, fell upon Jerusalem as Mary and Joseph came upon the young Christ poignantly preaching His Father's will. Her heart leapt to Him and flung itself in silent adoration at His feet.

Our Father, ten Hail Marys, Glory be to the Father.

Prayer Our Lady taught Jacinta to say after each decade.

O my Jesus, forgive us our sins, save us from the fires of hell, lead all souls to heaven, especially those in most need of Your mercy. Amen.

Hail, Holy Queen...

First Sorrowful Mystery

The Agony in the Garden

Resignation to the Will of God

Begin the Rosary with the Apostles' Creed, the Our Father and three Hail Marys.

The Sorrowful Mysteries

I — The Agony in the Garden

Beneath the light of the moon there is a lonely Man kneeling, His eyes dripping blood as He leans against a rock. Three who could help are sleeping close by. But the angels rush in to comfort Him.

Our Father, ten Hail Marys, Glory be to the Father.

Prayer Our Lady taught Jacinta to say after each decade.

O my Jesus, forgive us our sins, save us from the fires of hell, lead all souls to heaven, especially those in most need of Your mercy. Amen.

Second Sorrowful Mystery

The Scourging at the Pillar

To obtain the spirit of purity

II — The Scourging at the Pillar

Was it for this He gave up the carpenter's job and went forth to make His dream come true? Brutal, bloody blows pierce the strong flesh and break the brawny sinews as He accepts man's fulfillment of a God's dream.

Our Father, ten Hail Marys, Glory be to the Father.

Prayer Our Lady taught Jacinta to say after each decade.

O my Jesus, forgive us our sins, save us from the fires of hell, lead all souls to heaven, especially those in most need of Your mercy. Amen.

Third Sorrowful Mystery

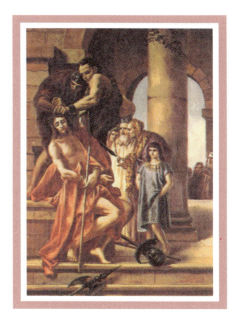

The Crowning with Thorns

To obtain moral courage

III — The Crowning with Thorns

The crown is cruelly close. It clings intimately to the candid brow, crushing intolerably through the disordered hair. Its jewels are clotted blood, mined from the agony of rejected love.

Our Father, ten Hail Marys, Glory be to the Father.

Prayer Our Lady taught Jacinta to say after each decade.

O my Jesus, forgive us our sins, save us from the fires of hell, lead all souls to heaven, especially those in most need of Your mercy. Amen.

Fourth Sorrowful Mystery

The Carrying of the Cross

To obtain patience in adversity

IV — The Carrying of the Cross

Eternity stumbles; God falls, red lips kissing the mud. He does not thrust the cross away, but clings to it even in the fall. His wistful eyes blood-filled, He takes the cross blindly, and through the silver-green light of a spring-scented morning, Christ staggers eternally forward.

Our Father, ten Hail Marys, Glory be to the Father.

Prayer Our Lady taught Jacinta to say after each decade.

O my Jesus, forgive us our sins, save us from the fires of hell, lead all souls to heaven, especially those in most need of Your mercy. Amen.

Fifth Sorrowful Mystery

The Crucifixion

To obtain sorrow for sin

V — The Crucifixion

Torn and stricken is the lithe body, pierced by crooked wounds, muddled with bronze dust; yet the little trees throw great shadows over Him, spring breathes a kiss against the bleeding knees, and one lone frightened bird, shamed by man's cruelty, flutters near the Heart, the loneliest Heart in all the world.

Our Father, ten Hail Marys, Glory be to the Father.

Prayer Our Lady taught Jacinta to say after each decade.

O my Jesus, forgive us our sins, save us from the fires of hell, lead all souls to heaven, especially those in most need of Your mercy. Amen.

Hail, Holy Queen...

First Glorious Mystery

The Resurrection

To obtain an increase of Faith

Begin the Rosary with the Apostles' Creed, the Our Father and three Hail Marys.

The Glorious Mysteries

I — The Resurrection

Before the sun danced on the Lake of Galilee, before day opened the folded fingers of dawn—suddenly He was there in the garden, He Who had been wounded five times unto death was alive and strong, His eyes two secret joys, His hair blown gold, His beauty shaming the beauty of the lilies.

And near the tomb was a riven stone, the quick whisper of winds, and the sound of a low-throated "Rabboni!" as peace entered the empty heart of the world.

Our Father, ten Hail Marys, Glory be to the Father.

Prayer Our Lady taught Jacinta to say after each decade.

O my Jesus, forgive us our sins, save us from the fires of hell, lead all souls to heaven, especially those in most need of Your mercy. Amen.

Second Glorious Mystery

The Ascension

To obtain an increase of Hope

II — The Ascension

He went up from Olivet, the mount of sorrow, now become a green-gold hill of joy. He blessed the sad earth, His hands trailing dream dust, and the apostles, flung to their knees, looked up from the tawny dust of an eastern hill to the bright glory of the place He has prepared for those who love Him.

Our Father, ten Hail Marys, Glory be to the Father.

Prayer Our Lady taught Jacinta to say after each decade.

O my Jesus, forgive us our sins, save us from the fires of hell, lead all souls to heaven, especially those in most need of Your mercy. Amen.

Third Glorious Mystery

The Descent of the Holy Spirit
To obtain an increase of Love

III — The Descent of the Holy Spirit

It was the tenth day after the Ascension. A quick movement stirred the quiet of the Cenacle as the Comforter came with the sound of a mighty wind. Glory flamed in the air; tongues of fire brightened the darkness. There was a promise of peace and strength. The twelve went forth to preach the Gospel, forth to suffering unafraid, their feet shod with the white Fire of the Holy Spirit.

Our Father, ten Hail Marys, Glory be to the Father.

Prayer Our Lady taught Jacinta to say after each decade.

O my Jesus, forgive us our sins, save us from the fires of hell, lead all souls to heaven, especially those in most need of Your mercy. Amen.

Fourth Glorious Mystery

The Assumption

To obtain devotion to Mary

IV — The Assumption

A paradox of death that was not dissolution, but the love tryst of the Virgin and her Son, such was Mary's Assumption. One last little breath, one flutter of her heart in joy, and she flung herself, through His almighty power, from the emptiness of earth past the outer-most lane of stars straight into the eternal embrace of God.

Our Father, ten Hail Marys, Glory be to the Father.

Prayer Our Lady taught Jacinta to say after each decade.

O my Jesus, forgive us our sins, save us from the fires of hell, lead all souls to heaven, especially those in most need of Your mercy. Amen.

Fifth Glorious Mystery

The Crowning of Mary

To obtain the grace of perseverance

V — The Crowning of Mary

Queen of all queens—thus was Mary crowned. The wings of angels trailed and flamed in the air; music trembled over the stars and beyond the sunset; seraphim folded the white petals of their souls in homage of her beauty. God crowned her Queen of Heaven and her brow was bound with stars.

Our Father, ten Hail Marys, Glory be to the Father.

Prayer Our Lady taught Jacinta to say after each decade.

O my Jesus, forgive us our sins, save us from the fires of hell, lead all souls to heaven, especially those in most need of Your mercy. Amen.

Hail, Holy Queen...

The Five First Saturdays

At each apparition Our Lady spoke of reparation. At the third apparition, July 13, 1917, she made the recommendation of the devotion to her Immaculate Heart through the First Saturdays of each month. On that occasion she said the following words to Lucy:

"Behold my heart surrounded with the thorns which ungrateful men place therein at every moment by their blasphemies and ingratitude. You at least try to console me and tell them that I promise to help at the hour of death with the graces needed for salvation, whoever on the First Saturday of five consecutive months, shall confess and receive Holy Communion, recite five decades of the Rosary, and keep me company for fifteen minutes while meditating on the fifteen mysteries of the Rosary, with the intention of making reparation to me."

This is known as the Great Promise of Our Lady of Fatima to those who sincerely attend Mass on the First Saturdays of each month.

The

WAY

of the

CROSS

In Short Form

Preparatory Prayer

O Merciful Jesus! With a contrite heart and penitent spirit I undertake this devotion of The Way of the Cross in honor of Your bitter sufferings and death.

I give humble thanks for the boundless love which impelled You to carry the Cross for me, an unworthy sinner, and to die for my redemption.

Make me worthy to gain all the spiritual benefits which are granted for this holy exercise.

I offer them to You in satisfaction for my sins, for which I am heartily sorry, for the consolation of the souls in Purgatory and for the grace to persevere in the pathways of virtue.

Act of Contrition

O my God! I am heartily sorry for having offended You, and I detest all my sins, because they have offended You, my God, Who are all good, and deserving of all my love. I firmly resolve, with the help of Your grace, to sin no more, and to avoid the near occasion of sin. Amen.

Pause briefly for silent reflection after reading the meditation for each station.

First Station

V. We adore You, O Christ, and we bless You.
R. Because by Your holy Cross You have redeemed the world!

Jesus bleeding from Head to Foot offers Himself to His enemies to be led to the most terrible death for me. Think of the love He has for my soul! How much value do I place on my own soul? God thought it worthy of the redeeming death of Christ.

+ + +

Our Father, Hail Mary and Glory be to the Father.

First Station

Jesus before Pilate

He was silent

Second Station

V. **We adore You, O Christ, and we bless You.**
R. **Because by Your holy Cross You have redeemed the world!**

Jesus gladly accepts the Cross to which His Hands and Feet will be nailed. Do I accept willingly my heaviest cross? What is it? My God, I touch my cross to Your Cross. Help me to carry it patiently. I am mindful that if anyone will follow You, he must be a cross-bearer.

Our Father, Hail Mary and Glory be to the Father.

Second Station

Jesus Is Laden with the Cross

He was resigned

Third Station

**V. We adore You, O Christ, and we bless You.
R. Because by Your holy Cross You have redeemed the world!**

  Jesus willed that His human nature should fall under the weight of His Cross. He wished to teach me that without His help I shall fall into sin. My Jesus, give strength to my weakness and save me from again committing my predominate sin of (   ).

Our Father, Hail Mary and Glory be to the Father.

Third Station

Jesus Falls the First Time

He was exhausted

Fourth Station

V. **We adore You, O Christ, and we bless You.**
R. **Because by Your holy Cross You have redeemed the world!**

Mary had always been close to her Divine Son. After a brief separation she risks her life to be with Him again. How much do I inconvenience myself to go to Confession and Holy Communion after days of separation from Jesus? These sacraments keep me close to God.

Our Father, Hail Mary and Glory be to the Father.

Fourth Station

Jesus Meets His Blessed Mother

He was sorrowful

Fifth Station

V. We adore You, O Christ, and we bless You.
R. Because by Your holy Cross You have redeemed the world!

Simon of Cyrene does his part to lessen the sufferings of Christ. Do I, by my good example and by prayer, try to prevent another from saying or doing the wrong thing, which would add to the sorrows of the Sacred Heart? My Savior, give me the grace to do my tiny share in lightening the burden of Your heavy Cross.

Our Father, Hail Mary and Glory be to the Father.

An Illustrated Book of Devotions **115**

Fifth Station

Simon of Cyrene Carries the Cross of Jesus

He was grateful

Sixth Station

V. We adore You, O Christ, and we bless You.
R. Because by Your holy Cross You have redeemed the world!

The woman whom we call Veronica fearlessly fought her way through the mob to the bleeding Savior in order to do Him a service. What good turn do I do every day for Christ? Henceforth I shall be more thoughtful. I sow in this life; I reap in the next.

Our Father, Hail Mary and Glory be to the Father.

Sixth Station

Veronica Wipes the Face of Jesus

He was compassionate

Seventh Station

V. **We adore You, O Christ, and we bless You.**
R. **Because by Your holy Cross You have redeemed the world!**

      Increasing weakness caused Jesus to fall the second time; but He also desires to teach me that I shall fall again and again unless I avoid temptation and seek strength in prayer and the Sacraments. Although never tempted beyond my strength, I am a weakling without the support of God's grace.

Our Father, Hail Mary and Glory be to the Father.

Seventh Station

Jesus Falls the Second Time

He was destitute

Eighth Station

V. **We adore You, O Christ, and we bless You.**
R. **Because by Your holy Cross You have redeemed the world!**

How little Jesus thought of Himself in His sufferings! He is willing to endure agony without murmur if those for whom He suffers will only learn the lesson that their sins have caused that agony. He was bruised for our iniquities. He was wounded for our sins. What sin of mine has grieved Christ most?

Our Father, Hail Mary and Glory be to the Father.

Eighth Station

Jesus Consoles the Women of Jerusalem

He was sympathetic

Ninth Station

V. We adore You, O Christ, and we bless You.
R. Because by Your holy Cross You have redeemed the world!

How many times have I taken resolutions to avoid my predominant sin, and to do some definite good work? How long have I kept my resolutions? Jesus falling for the third time, give me strength to rise above my weakness, and to walk with You until the end.

Our Father, Hail Mary and Glory be to the Father.

Ninth Station

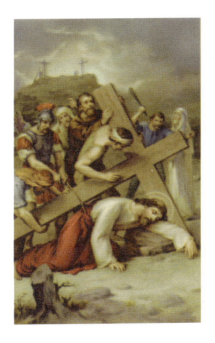

Jesus Falls the Third Time

He was crushed

Tenth Station

V. We adore You, O Christ, and we bless You.
R. Because by Your holy Cross You have redeemed the world!

Jesus atones, in this station, for our sins of immodesty. In what way do I offend most against modesty — by the eye, the ear, the tongue, by dress, by action? Jesus offers up His Body to repair the insults these sins offer to His Father. My Savior, help me to be always on guard so that my heart and soul may remain fitting abodes for Your presence.

Our Father, Hail Mary and Glory be to the Father.

Tenth Station

Jesus Is Stripped of His Garments

He was lonely

Eleventh Station

**V. We adore You, O Christ, and we bless You.
R. Because by Your holy Cross You have redeemed the world!**

After a siege of the most terrible suffering, the Master is fastened by nails to His deathbed. Good Jesus, bless me with Your outstretched hands. Let but one drop of blood from Your wounded palms fall on my soul and cleanse it from every sin. Grant that my life hereafter may be free from the guilt of Your suffering.

Our Father, Hail Mary and Glory be to the Father.

Eleventh Station

Jesus Is Nailed to the Cross

He was slain

Twelfth Station

V. **We adore You, O Christ, and we bless You.**
R. **Because by Your holy Cross You have redeemed the world!**

At the foot of Your Cross, O dying Christ, I ask pardon for the part I have had in Your death. I am heartily sorry for all my sins. Be with me, Divine Redeemer, in my last moments, forgive me as You forgave the penitent thief and receive my soul into Paradise forever.

Our Father, Hail Mary and Glory be to the Father.

Twelfth Station

Jesus Dies on the Cross

He was loyal

Thirteenth Station

V. **We adore You, O Christ, and we bless You.**
R. **Because by Your holy Cross You have redeemed the world!**

    O Mary, Mother of Jesus and my Mother, let me kneel with you beside the lifeless Body of your beloved Son. Obtain for me the grace to be loyal to Him by walking in the way of His commandments. Obtain for me especially the grace to receive Him worthily in Holy Communion until I am united with Him and you for all eternity.

Our Father, Hail Mary and Glory be to the Father.

Thirteenth Station

Jesus Is Taken Down From the Cross

He was helpless

Fourteenth Station

**V. We adore You, O Christ, and we bless You.
R. Because by Your holy Cross You have redeemed the world!**

Jesus taught me how to live and how to die. He reminds me now that if I stay close to Him in life and in death, I shall rise from the tomb, as He did, glorious and immortal, and share the happiness of Heaven with Him for all eternity. Grant me the grace, good Master, so to live on earth that I may be worthy to share Your glory forever and ever.

Our Father, Hail Mary and Glory be to the Father.

Lamb of God Who takes away the sins of the world, have mercy on me.

Say the Our Father, the Hail Mary, and the Glory be to the Father five times for the intention of the Sovereign Pontiff.

Fourteenth Station

Jesus Is Laid in the Tomb

He was at rest

Concluding Prayer

Almighty and eternal God, merciful Father, Who have given Your only-begotten Son to the human race as an example of humility, obedience and patience, and have ordained that He carry the Cross and precede us on the way of life; grant, we beseech You, that inflamed by His infinite love we may take upon ourselves the sweet yoke of His Gospel and the mortification of the Cross, following Him as His true disciples, so that we may one day gloriously rise with Him in the blessed eternity of the Kingdom of Heaven.

The Perpetual Novena in honor of Our Lady of the Miraculous Medal

(Lourdes Hymn)

Immaculate Mary,
Your praises we sing,
Who reigns now in splendor
with Jesus, our King.

Chorus

Ave, Ave, Ave, Maria!
Ave, Ave, Maria!

Your name is our power,
Your virtues our light,
Your love is our comfort,
Your pleading our light.

Chorus

Reading of Announcements and Favors

Opening Prayer

Priest: In the name of the Father and of the Son and of the Holy Spirit.
People: Amen.

Priest: Come, Holy Spirit, fill the hearts of Your faithful, and kindle in them the fire of Your love. Send forth Your Spirit, and they shall be created.
People: And You shall renew the face of the earth.
Priest: Let us pray.

O God, who instructed the hearts of the faithful by the light of the Holy Spirit, grant us in the same Spirit to be truly wise and ever to rejoice in His consolation, through Jesus Christ our Lord.
People: Amen.
Priest: O Mary, conceived without sin,
People: Pray for us who have recourse to you. (3 times.)
Priest and People: O Lord Jesus Christ, who have vouchsafed to glorify by numberless miracles the Blessed Virgin Mary, immaculate from the first moment of her conception, grant that all who devoutly implore her protection on earth, may eternally enjoy Your presence in heaven, who, with the Father and Holy Spirit, live and reign, God, for ever and ever. Amen.

O Lord Jesus Christ, who for the accomplishment of Your greatest works, have chosen the weak things of the world, that no flesh may glory in Your sight; and who for a better and more widely diffused belief in the Immaculate Conception of Your Mother, have wished that the Miraculous Medal be manifested to Saint Catherine Labouré, grant, we beseech You, that filled with like humility, we may glorify this mystery by word and work. Amen.

Memorare

Priest and People:

Remember, O most compassionate Virgin Mary, that never was it known that anyone who fled to your protection, implored your help, or sought your intercession, was left unaided. Inspired with this confidence, we fly unto you, O Virgin of Virgins, our Mother; to you we come; before you we kneel sinful and sorrowful. O Mother of the Word Incarnate, despise not our petitions, but in your mercy hear and answer them. Amen.

Novena Prayer

Priest and People:

O Immaculate Virgin Mary, Mother of Our Lord Jesus and our Mother, penetrated with the most lively confidence in your all-powerful and never-failing intercession, manifested so often through the Miraculous Medal, we your loving and trustful children implore you to obtain for us the graces and favors we ask during this Novena, if they be beneficial to our immortal souls, and the souls for whom we pray. (Here privately form your petitions.) You know, O Mary, how often our souls have been the sanctuaries of your Son who hates iniquity. Obtain for us then a deep hatred of sin and that purity of heart which will attach us to God alone so that our every thought, word and deed may tend to His greater glory. Obtain for us also a spirit of prayer and self-denial that we may recover by penance what we have lost by sin and at length attain to that blessed abode where you are the Queen of angels and of men. Amen.

An Act of Consecration to Our Lady of the Miraculous Medal

Priest and People:

O Virgin Mother of God, Mary Immaculate, we dedicate and consecrate ourselves to you under the title of Our Lady of the Miraculous Medal. May this Medal be for each one of us a sure sign of your affection for us and a constant reminder of our duties toward you. Ever while wearing it, may we be blessed by your loving protection and preserved in the grace of your Son. O most powerful Virgin, Mother of our Savior, keep us close to you every moment of our lives. Obtain for us, your children, the grace of a happy death; so that, in union with you, we may enjoy the bliss of heaven forever. Amen.

Priest: O Mary, conceived without sin,

People: Pray for us who have recourse to you. (3 times.)

Benediction of the Blessed Sacrament

(NOTE: Diocesan regulations may dictate the use of another translation.)

Humbly let us voice our homage
>   For so great a sacrament,
Let all former rites surrender
>   To the Lord's New Testament;
What our senses fail to fathom
>   Let us grasp through faith's consent!
Glory, honor, adoration
>   Let us sing with one accord!
Praised be God, Almighty Father;
>   Praised be Christ, His Son, Our Lord;
Praised be God the Holy Spirit;
>   Triune Godhead be adored! Amen.

Let us Pray

Priest: God, who left us in this wondrous sacrament a memorial of Your Passion and death, help us, we beseech You, so to reverence the sacred mysteries of Your Body and Blood, that we may always experience the effects of Your Redemption. Who live and reign forever and ever.
People: Amen.

Hymn—Hail, Holy Queen Enthroned Above

(All seated)

Hail, holy Queen enthroned above,
O Maria.
Hail, Queen of mercy and of love,
O Maria.

Chorus

Triumph, all ye Cherubim,
Sing with us, ye Seraphim,
Heav'n and earth resound the hymn:
Salve, Salve, Salve Regina.
The cause of joy to men below,
O Maria.
The spring through which all graces flow,
O Maria. — *Chorus*

O gentle, loving, holy one,
O Maria.
The God of Light became your Son,
O Maria. — *Chorus*

The Divine Praises

Blessed be God.
Blessed be His holy Name.
Blessed be Jesus Christ, true God and true Man.
Blessed be the Name of Jesus.
Blessed be His Most Sacred Heart.
Blessed be His Most Precious Blood.
Blessed be Jesus in the most holy Sacrament of the Altar.
Blessed be the Holy Spirit, the Paraclete.
Blessed be the great Mother of God, Mary most holy.
Blessed be her holy and Immaculate Conception.
Blessed be her glorious Assumption.
Blessed be the name of Mary, Virgin and Mother.
Blessed be St. Joseph, her most chaste spouse.
Blessed be God in His angels and in His saints.

May the Heart of Jesus, in the Most Blessed Sacrament, be praised, adored and loved, with grateful affection, at every moment, in all the tabernacles of the world, even to the end of time. Amen.

Sing:
> O Mary, conceived without sin,
> Pray for us, pray for us,
> O Mary, conceived without sin,
> Pray for us, who have recourse to you.

The Chaplet of the Divine Mercy

(to be recited on ordinary Rosary beads)

Begin with:
> Our Father, Hail Mary, the Apostles' Creed.

Then, on the Our Father beads, say the following words:

> Eternal Father, I offer You the Body and Blood, Soul and Divinity of Your dearly beloved Son, Our Lord Jesus Christ, in atonement for our sins and those of the whole world.

On the Hail Mary beads, say the following words:

> For the sake of His sorrowful Passion, have mercy on us and on the whole world.

In conclusion, recite these words three times:

> Holy God, Holy Might One, Holy Immortal One, have mercy on us and on the whole world. (From the Diary of Blessed Faustina, 476).

> "Through the Chaplet you will obtain everything, if what you ask for will be compatible with My will" (Diary, 1731, 1541).

> "By the Novena of Chaplets before the Feast of Mercy, I will grant every possible grace to souls" (Diary, 796).

> "Even if a sinner were most hardened, if only once he will recite this Chaplet, he will obtain grace from My infinite mercy" (Diary, 687).